AIR WAR ARCHIVE

FOCKE-WULF Fw 200

THE LUFTWAFFE'S LONG RANGE MARITIME BOMBER

AIR WAR ARCHIVE

FOCKE-WULF Fw 200

THE LUFTWAFFE'S LONG RANGE MARITIME BOMBER

RARE LUFTWAFFE PHOTOGRAPHS FROM WARTIME COLLECTIONS

CHRIS GOSS

FRONTLINE
BOOKS

FOCKE-WULF Fw 200
The Luftwaffe's Long Range Maritime Bomber

First published in Great Britain in 2019 by Frontline Books,
an imprint of Pen & Sword Books Ltd,
Yorkshire – Philadelphia

ISBN: 978-1-84832-487-9

Typeset in 9.5/12pt Avenir by Aura Technology and Software Services, India
Printed and bound by CPI Group (UK) Ltd, Croydon CR0 4YY

Pen & Sword Books Ltd incorporates the imprints of Air World Books, Pen & Sword Archaeology, Atlas, Aviation, Battleground, Discovery, Family History, History, Maritime, Military, Naval, Politics, Social History, Transport, True Crime, Claymore Press, Frontline Books, Praetorian Press, Seaforth Publishing and White Owl

For a complete list of Pen & Sword titles please contact:

PEN & SWORD BOOKS LTD
47 Church Street, Barnsley, South Yorkshire, S70 2AS, UK.
E-mail: enquiries@pen-and-sword.co.uk
Website: www.pen-and-sword.co.uk

Or

PEN AND SWORD BOOKS,
1950 Lawrence Roadd, Havertown, PA 19083, USA
E-mail: Uspen-and-sword@casematepublishers.com
Website: www.penandswordbooks.com

CONTENTS

INTRODUCTION

Designed as a four-engine airliner, the Focke-Wulf Fw 200 first flew in July 1937. It was duly operated by Deutsche Luft Hansa as well as Det Danske Luftfahrtselskab Danish Airlines and the Brazilian Syndicato Condor. Its ability to fly passengers long distance was quickly proven in 1938 with flights to Cairo, then New York and finally Tokyo. Such flights impressed the Japanese who placed orders for five civil versions and one military.

By September 1939, Hauptmann Edgar Petersen had begun to champion the formation of a very long-range maritime reconnaissance unit. The only aircraft capable of meeting this task was the Fw 200. In October 1939, he was appointed commander of a six-aircraft Fernaufklärungsstaffel (Long Range Reconnaissance Squadron) which later became I Gruppe/Kampfgeschwader 40 (I/KG 40).

The Condor, as the Fw 200 became known, was soon in action in the Norway Campaign from April 1940 onwards. The first Condor loss during a combat mission occurred on 22 April 1940 – probably due to weather or mechanical failure – and just over a month later another was shot down by an RAF fighter. By the end of the Norwegian campaign, the Condor, with I/KG 40 having lost just one more Fw 200 to fighters, had proved its worth.

The Luftwaffe was soon undertaking mining and reconnaissance missions around Britain and felt confident to use the Condor for this purpose. However, on the night of 20 July 1940, a Condor was shot down by anti-aircraft fire when it strayed too close to the British mainland whilst dropping mines and four nights later another suffered engine failure and ditched in the Irish Sea. Such missions soon stopped as such a loss rate could not be endured when Focke-Wulf was only capable of manufacturing just three Condors per month.

So, in August 1940 I/KG 40 found itself at Bordeaux-Mérignac in south-western France, where, far from the attention of RAF fighters, the crews were able to fly armed reconnaissance missions with little fear of being shot down, preying on undefended merchant ships and at the same time acting as the Kriegsmarine's eyes and ears over the Atlantic.

By 31 December 1940, the Gruppe had been credited with sinking in the region of 800,000 tons of shipping for the loss of just two Condors in accidents on operational sorties. The Condor and its crews had quickly made a name for themselves, exemplified by the attack on the 42,500-ton troop ship *Empress of Britain* on 26 October 1940. By early 1941, I/KG 40 already had five Knight's Cross winners.

With the escalation of the war in the Atlantic, the future for the Condor looked positive especially with them being detached to northern Norway to fly missions off the Faeroes, Iceland and even the shipping lanes approaching Ireland. Losses were still mainly as a result of flak or accident, operations for the first half of 1941 mounting to five to flak, one to an enemy aircraft and three to unknown causes. These were hard to sustain because, for example, as of April 1941, there were only twenty-five to thirty Condors and of these, no more than six to eight were serviceable at any one time. The machine was particularly prone to mechanical problems and structural failure, something that plagued it throughout its life. Nevertheless, to lessen the risk, in November 1941, it was decreed that the practice of low-level attacks be abandoned and crews had to rely on the superior Lotfe 7 bomb sight to attack from altitude and relative safety.

Out over the Atlantic, the Condors of I/KG 40 continued to be a menace to Allied shipping. In the first two months of 1941, Condors had a hand in sinking in the region of thirty-nine ships and about seventeen from March to July 1941 but just four were sunk or badly damaged by Condors during the last five months of 1941. Condors were now being prevented from attacking ships by improved defences and were relegated to shadowing duties. A number of merchant ships, such as the 8,000 ton *Maplin* had been converted to Fighter Catapult ships, equipped with 'launch and forget' fighters, the first victory being on 3 August 1941 when a Hurricane claimed to have shot down a Condor before the pilot baled out and was rescued – the Condor ditched off the French coast. An additional defensive measure was the introduction of the escort carrier HMS *Audacity* at the end of 1941 but only three Condors can be attributed to aircraft flying from this carrier before *Audacity* was sunk by a U-boat on 21 December 1941.

From the start of 1942, the U-boat war had escalated following America joining the war. I/KG 40 had now moved north to Trondheim-Vaernes in Norway in March 1942 in support of the northern U-boat war and attacks against Arctic convoys. At the same time, III/KG 40 had finished converting from the Heinkel 111 to the Condor and was now operating from Bordeaux. 1942 would also see a temporary change in role for the Condor when it was used at the end of the year to re-supply the Afrika Korps and to support German ground troops at Stalingrad. Both tasks had finished by February 1943.

All this time, the Condor was being modified. Put simply, the pre-war A and B versions became the C-0 in 1939 (cowling, propeller and undercarriage modifications), then the C-1 (increased armament), C-2 (bomb racks, engine and internal modifications), C-3 (engine, structural strengthening, bomb load and defensive armament being the major changes). Later versions were the C-4 (air-to-surface radar & defensive armament), C-5 (transport and trials), C-6 (modified to carry missiles), C-7 (believed to be transport) and finally the C-8 (as the C-6, ventral gondola lengthened).

With the Atlantic U-boat war continuing and the numbers of Allied ships and, more importantly, aircraft increasing, Condor attrition was rising – I and III/KG 40 would lose in the region of twenty-six Condors in 1942 and about forty-two in 1943. Nevertheless, there were still some spectacular successes. On 11 July 1943, the former luxury passenger liner and now troopship *California*, together with *Duchess of York* and *Port Fairy* were attacked by Condors which sank *California* and *Duchess of York* and damaged *Port Fairy*. However, such successes were few and far between and as Allied superiority increased, the supply of Condors began to dwindle.

By the Summer of 1943, the Luftwaffe had two air-launched guided weapons for anti-shipping operations, one of which was the Henschel Hs 293 which could be launched from with Condor. Several Fw 200 C-3s and C-4s were converted to carry one on each wing outboard of the outer engine nacelles. Such aircraft were designated Fw 200 C-6 but the Fw 200 C-8 was designed specifically as a launch platform for the Hs 293. However, the first mission using the Hs 293 was not flown until 28 December 1943.

The new year of 1944 started badly when another attack on Bordeaux-Mérignac resulted in the destruction of a suggested eight Condors with another three damaged. At the same time Condors began to fall prey to RAF and American long-range fighters over land as opposed to the seas. The end of March/start of April 1944 saw the last major combat between Condors of KG 40 and Allied aircraft with three Condors shot down by carrier fighters attacking Convoy JW 58/RA58 sailing from Scotland to Russia.

It was clear that Condors could no longer keep operating. On 20 March 1944, III/KG 40 reported that of the thirty-five aircraft on strength, only eight were serviceable and three months later, this had reduced to twenty-three on strength but twelve serviceable. From April 1944 onwards, Condor losses on operations fell to zero but many were still being lost in accident or falling victim to intruding Allied aircraft. Unable to operate over the Atlantic from French bases following the Allied invasion of Normandy on 6 June 1944, the following month, the decision was made to withdraw Condors from France to either Norway or to Germany and Austria. From now on, they were used entirely in the transport role as it was all but impossible to carry out effective combat sorties with any guarantee of success or even landing safely.

November 1944 would see KG 40 disbanded (in preparation for the formation of the Messerschmitt 262-equipped KG (Jagd) 40) and its aircraft, aircrew and groundcrew dispersed to other air or units or the aircraft grounded. 8/KG 40 became Transportfliegerstaffel Condor while some aircraft were transferred to 14/Transportgeschwader 4 at Wiener-Neustadt in Austria.

At the end of the war, Condors were found abandoned at airfields all over Europe. Of particular interest were the Condors of Fliegerstaffel des Führers, used by senior political and military personages from Hitler downwards. However, with no potential post-war use, these, and all other Condors, were scrapped.

Showing the elegant lines of the Condor, this is Fw 200 C-1 coded F8+DK, which is believed to be Wk Nr 0003 that force-landed in Portugal on 9 February 1941.

Pictured by a photographer from Focke-Wulf on 17 January 1941, this aircraft is Wk Nr 0043 which was coded SG+KS. Other images from the same series feature later in the book.

GLOSSARY AND ABBREVIATIONS

AA	Anti-aircraft
Adj	Adjutant
Aufklärungsgruppe	Reconnaissance Wing
Bordfunker	Radio Operator
Beobachter	Observer
Bordmechaniker	Flight Engineer
Bordschütz	Air Gunner
Deutsches Kreuz in Gold	German Cross in Gold award (DKiG)
Ehrenpokal (Pokal)	Goblet of Honour-awarded for outstanding achievements in the air war
Eiserne Kreuz	Iron Cross (came in First an Second Class)
Ergänzungs	Training
Feldwebel	Flight Sergeant
Fern	Long range
Flak	Anti-aircraft
Flieger	Aircraftman
Fliegerführer Atlantik	Air Commander for the Atlantic region
Fluzeugführer	Pilot
Frontflugspange	Mission Clasp-awarded for operational flights
Führer	Leader
Gefreiter	Leading Aircraftman
Generalfeldmarschall	Air Chief Marshal
Geschwader	Group consisting three Gruppen commanded by a Geschwader Kommodore (Gesch Komm)
Gruppe (Gr)	Wing consisting three Staffeln; commanded by a Gruppen Kommandeur (Gr Kdr). Gruppe number denoted by Roman numerals (e.g II).

Hauptmann	Flight Lieutenant/Captain
Ia	Operations Officer
Ju	Junkers
Kampfgeschwader (KG)	Bomber Group
Kampfgeschwader zur besonderen Verwendung (KGzbV)	Normal designation for a transport unit
Kette	Three aircraft tactical formation similar to RAF vic
Kriegsmarine	German Navy
Leutnant	Pilot Officer/2nd Lt
Luftflotte	Air Fleet
Major	Squadron Leader/Major
Me	Messerschmitt (used by RAF)
Nachtrichtenoffizier	Communications Officer
Oberfeldwebel	Warrant Officer
Obergefreiter	Senior Aircraftman/Cpl
Oberleutnant	Flying Officer/1st Lt
Oberst	Group Captain/Colonel
Oberstleutnant	Wing Commander/Lt Col
Reichsmarschall	Marshal of the Air Force
Ritterkreuz	Knight's Cross
Ritterkreuz mit Eichenlaub	Knight's Cross with Oakleaves
Stab	Staff or HQ; formation in which Gr Kdr and Gesch Komm flew.
Stabsfeldwebel	Senior Warrant Officer
Staffel	Squadron (12 aircraft); commanded by a Staffel Kapitän. Staffel number denoted by Arabic numerals (eg.2)
Unteroffizier	Sergeant
Werk Nummer (Wk Nr)	Serial Number

ACKNOWLEDGEMENTS

I would like to thank the following for their assistance in compiling this book: Justin Horgan (Ireland), Tony Kearns (Ireland), Eggert Norâdahl (Iceland), Tim Oliver (UK), Günther Ott (Germany), Gianandrea Bussi (Italy), Bernd Rauchbach (Germany), Robert Forsyth (UK), and Juan-Carlos Salgado (Spain).

PART I

1939–1940

Fw 200 A-0 *Werk Nummer* (Wk Nr) 3098 D-ACVH named *Grenzmark* in Deutsche Luft Hansa (DLH) markings showing the clean lines of the airliner. This aircraft became NK+NM and was assigned to Fliegerstaffel Der Führers (FdF). It was lost in an accident at Orel on 23 November 1941.

Fw 200 V3 Wk Nr 3099 carried a number of codes in its service. Initially D-ARHU and named *Ostmark*, it later became D-2600, WL-2600 and 26-00 and was renamed *Immelmann III* whilst serving with FdF. It would be destroyed in an air raid on 18 July 1944.

The first military Condor to suffer an incident was Fw 200 V10 Wk Nr 0001 coded BS+AF. Originally coded D-ASHH and named *Hessen*, it was assigned to Oberstleutnant Theodor Rowehl's Versuchsstelle für Höhenflug, part of Aufklärungsgruppe Oberbefehlshaber der Luftwaffe. Converted to carry cameras and with an increased fuel capacity, it suffered engine failure on take-off from Jever in northern Germany on 23 November 1939, when heading for a reconnaissance mission to Iceland and the Faeroes. Flugkapitän Martin Königs and his crew were all uninjured, but the aircraft suffered fifty per cent damage.

Condor Wk Nr 0002, with the codes BS+AG, was originally built as the second B-1 airliner for DLH but in September 1939 it was ordered by the Luftwaffe to be delivered as the C-1 series prototype V11. After intensive testing by Erprobungsstelle Rechlin and Tarnewitz, it was assigned to 1/KG 40 on 20 April 1940. This photograph is taken at the Focke-Wulf factory at Bremen – note the other Condor fuselage in the background.

An earlier photograph of Wk Nr 0002 (just visible on the nose) minus the A Stand front dorsal gun position. This aircraft was coded BS+AG and it is the censor that has removed the dorsal gun position.

An interesting side view of C-1 Wk Nr 0005, coded BS+AJ, showing the ventral gondola and a lack of upper gun positions. These are absent because this was the first photograph released showing a military Condor and the censor has deleted both dorsal gun positions and the bomb racks outside the engine. This aircraft was handed over to 1/KG 40 at Bremen on 5 April 1940.

Opposite above: On 28 May 1940, Fw 200 C-1 coded F8+AH of 1/KG 40 is understood to have force-landed at Gardemoen; it is believed that this is that aircraft being towed away by two Panzer IIs. Note the A Stand under the tarpaulin and the newly-adopted KG 40 'World in a Ring' emblem.

Opposite below: Another casualty which is believed to have occurred at Gardemoen on 28 May 1940, was Fw 200 V2 Wk Nr 2824, GF+GC, named *Westfalen*. It arrived on 1./KG 40, from VfH, on 28 November 1939. It became a training and courier aircraft and was coded F8+GH. In March 1940 it was attached to 4/KGzbv 107.

This is believed to be the first F8+EH to serve with 1/KG 40. On 31 July 1940, Fw 200 C-2 Wk Nr 0023, coded F8+EH, arrived on 1/KG 40, apparently a replacement for this Fw 200 C-1 Wk Nr 0007, F8+EH, which was shot down by flak into the North Sea off Hartlepool during a mine-laying mission on the night of 20 July. Hauptmann Roman Steszyn (St Kap), Feldwebel Willi Meyer, Gefreiter Silverius Zraunig and Gefreiter Josef Perl were all killed, whilst Feldwebel Herbert Külken and Feldwebel Karl Nicolai survived and were taken prisoner.

Below and opposite: Three views of F8+BH of 1/KG 40 during target practice on a land range. The aircraft is bombing from low level.

Opposite above: This Fw 200 of 1/KG 40 is about to take off on a mission laden with a 500kg bomb; the pilot of this aircraft is Hauptmann Edmund Daser (middle), the Staffel Kapitän of 1/KG 40. Dropping of 500kg bombs was recorded against Liverpool and Birkenhead by small numbers of Condors at the end of August 1940.

The results of one such attack. This is the SS *Starstone* which was attacked by Feldwebel Bernhard Flinsch of 2/KG 40 in F8+BK at 11.00 hours on 31 October 1940, 300 kilometres west of Achill Head. His crew dropped two 250kg bombs, damaging the 5,700-ton cargo ship.

This Condor shows twenty-eight missions and nine shipping successes, recorded on 25 August 1940, 15 September 1940 (2), 30 October 1940, 6 November 1940 (3) and 15 November 1940 (2). It is probable that this aircraft was flown by Hauptmann Edmund Daser, the Staffel Kapitän of 1/KG 40.

PART II
1941

Above and opposite: The first in a series of photographs that were taken by a photographer from Focke-Wulf on 17 January 1941. This aircraft is Wk Nr 0043 – the last two digits are just visible on the nose – which was coded SG+KS.

SG
XS
K
S

This is Fw 200 C-3 Wk Nr 0042, which is coded SG+KR. Again, the censor has doctored the gun position. This aircraft was lost on 5 February 1941, as F8+AH of 1./KG 40, when it crashed near Durrus in County Cork.

Opposite above: It is noticeable that in the pictures of SG+KS that were taken on 17 January 1941, no A Stand can be seen - probably deleted by the censor.

Opposite below: A fourth view of SG+KS. When serving with Stab I/KG 40, it had been modified to be a C-3/U2 variant, coded F8+AB.

Closest to the camera is a Fw 200 C-3, that coded F8+GH, of 1/KG 40 whilst in the background is a Fw 200 A-0, this one coded F8+EU. Although it cannot be stated conclusively, F8+GH could be Fw 200 C-3/U4 Wk Nr 0074, which flew from Mérignac to Athens-Eleusis on 26 August 1941 and was then lost on 5 September. It crashed into the sea south of Fleves, Greece, due to engine problems, killing Oberleutnant Horst Neumann and his crew. The intake on the upper fuselage is for the Kärcher Heizung cabin heating system. F8+EU is Wk Nr 2895, formerly D-ARHW *Friesland*/CB+FA of 10 (Erg)/KG 40 which was being used for resupply as well as crew training at this time.

Opposite above: A final view of SG+KS. This aircraft suffered a direct hit by flak whilst attacking Convoy OB 346 on 18 July 1941. Ritterkreuz holder and Gruppen Kommandeur Hauptmann Fritz Fliegel and his crew (Leutnant Wolf-Dietrich Kadelke, Feldwebel Hans Rottke, Gefreiter Karl Becker, Unteroffizier Johann Kothe and Unteroffizier Karl Maurer) were all killed.

Opposite below: Fw 200 C-3 Wk Nr 0046, coded F8+EL, was with 3/KG 40 from 19 March to 9 July 1941 when, flown by Leutnant Robert Maly, it suffered thirty per cent damage landing at Cognac due to a technical fault. After repair, it was re-coded F8+FL, then transferred to III/KG 40 and finally abandoned in Russia on 16 January 1943 whilst flying with KGzbV 200. Note what appears to be mission marks on the tail beneath the swastika and kill markings on the rudder.

A Fw 200 C-3, coded F8+CH, in a blast pen at Mérignac, early 1941. Two kill markings on the rudder and a series of mission marks on the tail indicate this aircraft could be Wk Nr 0026. On 16 January 1941, Hauptmann Konrad Verlohr was involved in the sinking of the SS *Onoba* and SS *Meandros*. On 24 July of that year, Verlohr, by now St Kap of 1/KG 40, was reported missing in this aircraft together with Leutnant Walter Gröner, Oberfeldwebel Henry Rasquin, Unteroffizier Hans Zeitler, Feldwebel Walter Drost and Oberleutnant Paul Schlafke.

Opposite above: A Fw 200 C-3 of 1/KG 40. Early Condors on I/KG 40 had names of planets or constellations painted on the tip of the nose. In this case the name appears to have weathered, making it impossible to read. Known names are *Atair*, *Mars* (F8+AB), *Wega* (F8+AK), *Deneb* (F8+AH and F8+DH), *Jupiter* (F8+BB), *Aries*, *Merkur*, *Polaris*, *Pollux*, *Elektra* (F8+EH), *Sirius* (F8+BK), *Artemis*, *Capella* (F8+CH), *Bellatrix*, *Orion* and *Neptun* (F8+DL).

Opposite below: A Condor of I/KG 40 pictured at the dispersal at Bordeaux-Mérignac in early 1941.

The RAF attacked Mérignac on a number of occasions in late 1940 and 1941 – this is the aftermath of one of raids. On 23 November 1940, for example, the attackers destroyed a C-3 (Wk Nr 0027) and a D-1 (Wk Nr 0009). This is believed to be the result of the 13 April 1941 attack which resulted in three Condors being destroyed.

Opposite: A Condor carries out a very low fly-by at Mérignac. Note the distinctive hangars and the operations building.

Another view of the aftermath of the attack on 13 April 1941.

Groundcrew loading 250kg bombs to a Condor of I/KG 40 at Mérignac. Note the open bomb doors in the ventral gondola. The name on the nose has evaded attempts to decipher it.

Above and opposite: Three pictures that depict groundcrew marshalling in a Fw 200 C-3 at Mérignac. The name on the nose is *Atair*, but it has not been possible to match a code or Staffel with this aircraft.

Condors of I/KG 40 pictured at dispersal at Mérignac in 1941. Nearest the camera is a C-3 of 3 Staffel, that coded F8+DL, which carries a number of mission marks on the tail. This aircraft is first recorded being flown operationally on 17 February 1941, on which occasion it was commanded by Oberleutnant Rudolf Mons. It had flown thirteen operational sorties by 12 April 1941. However, there is then no further record of an F8+DL until 7 August 1941. It is possible that this aircraft was Wk Nr 0033, which was destroyed in an air attack on Mérignac on 13 April 1941. Mons himself would later be awarded the Ritterkreuz and was killed in action, leading II/KG 40, on 26 November 1943.

Fw 200 C-3s parked up at Mérignac in the spring of 1941.

Loading a 250kg bomb onto a Condor at Mérignac, 1941.

Replacing MG 17s on a I/KG 40 Condor at Mérignac sometime during 1941.

Working on what appears to be a C-3, that coded F8+BL. There are a number of mission marks on the tail and possibly the top of the rudder. F8+BL is first mentioned as flying operationally on 6 February 1941.

Condor F8+FL taxies in at Mérignac in 1941. By the number of Kriegsmarine personnel waiting for this aircraft, it is probable that it is carrying a senior naval officer, many of whom visited KG 40 during its deployment to Mérignac.

A Rotte of Fw 200 C-4s of I/KG 40 in the late summer of 1941.

A visit by the Kommandant of the Luftkriegsakadamie to Mérignac, late 1940/early 1941.

Hauptmann Edmund Daser of 1/KG 40 speaking with the Kommandant of the Luftkriegsakadamie. Note the mixture of 50kg and 250kg practice bombs and the 20mm MG FF in the front of the ventral gondola. Daser would soon be awarded the Ritterkreuz; he survived the war.

A practice 250kg bomb marked up to commemorate the 1,000th dropped by I/KG 40.

An unidentified C-3 of I/KG 40 taxying in at Mérignac. Clearly visible are the bomb racks outside the outer engines and the Kärcher Heizung intake on the fuselage.

Opposite: The Kommandant of the Luftkriegsakadamie watches a 250kg practice bomb being loaded to a Condor.

Opposite above: A Fw 200 C-3 of I/KG 40 seen at Mérignac in the spring of 1941. Note the 20mm cannon in the ventral gondola and the Kärcher Heizung intake.

Opposite below: A Condor in the foreground at what is believed to be the Ritterkreuz award ceremony for Hauptmann Edmund Daser at Mérignac. He was awarded this coveted medal on 21 February 1941, for sinking a total of 68,000 tons of enemy shipping.

Pictured exiting from the crew door of a Fw 200 of 1/KG 40, that coded F8+BH, is believed to be Oberfeldwebel Paul Schmidt, First Bordfunker on Oberleutnant Hans Buchholz's crew. Buchholz would be awarded the Ritterkreuz on 24 March 1941. He was shot down by flak 300 miles west of Donegal Bay on 19 May 1941. At the time he was flying Fw 200 C-3, Wk Nr 0060, F8+DH. Both he and Schmidt were killed, whilst the remainder of the crew (Oberfeldwebel Otto Kroke, Unteroffizier Meinhard Milde, Oberfeldwebel Erich Kielke, Feldwebel Kurt Brattke and meteorologist Friedrich Keller) were captured.

Hauptmann Edmund Daser (centre) with two unidentified officers walking away from F8+CH, again in the spring of 1941. Note the mission markings at the base of the tail.

Opposite above: Another VIP visit to I/KG 40 at Mérignac in the spring of 1941. Note the sealant around the panel joints under the Condor's nose.

Opposite below: An unidentified C-3 of I/KG 40. Pictured minus a spinner on the port outer engine, it is possible that this is F8+GH of 1/KG 40.

Hauptmann Edmund Daser, second from left, wearing the Ritterkreuz. Note that the F8 of KG 40 has been painted over the manufacturer's code, which is almost visible.

Opposite: Three NCO members of Hauptmann Daser's crew sporting unusual headgear. It seems that censors have covered up the F8 codes on this aircraft.

Opposite: This is believed to be Hauptmann Bernhard Jope of 3/KG 40 taxing in at Mérignac on 21 February 1941 after two successful missions. The first saw him attack a convoy two days earlier, landing at Stavanger in Norway, and then attacking the same convoy on the return flight on 21 February. Jope can be seen looking out of the cockpit of his Condor in the second photograph. He would be awarded the Ritterkreuz mit Eichlenlaub and survived the war.

Oberleutnant Hans Buchholz of 1/KG 40 photographed on his return from a mission, early 1941. Buchholz would be awarded the Ritterkreuz; he was killed in action on 19 May of the same year.

Jope is seen reporting to the Gruppen Kommandeur, Hauptmann Fritz Fliegel. On 19 February 1941, Jope took off from Mérignac and attacked convoy OB287, sinking the tanker *Gracia* and cargo ship *Housatonic*. He then landed in Stavanger and took off again on 21 February 1941, attacking the same convoy en route to Mérignac, this time sinking the freighter *Scottish Standard*.

Bernhard Jope surrounded by members of I/KG 40. Just visible around his neck is the Ritterkreuz. To his left, wearing a forage cap, is Oberleutnant Heinrich Schlosser, whilst the officer also on his left with the peaked cap is believed to be Leutnant Robert Maly. Ahead of Jope is Hauptmann Fritz Fliegel. Schlosser was later awarded the Ritterkreuz and survived the war.

Opposite above: Just hidden behind the unidentified officer pouring the champagne is Oberleutnant Ernst Hetzel who was later awarded the Ritterkreuz and survived the war. Facing the camera are Hauptmann Kern, Hauptmann Fliegel and Leutnant Burkard.

Opposite below: Seen from left to right are Oberleutnant Ernst Hetzel, Oberleutnant Hans Buchholz, Hauptmann Kern and Hauptmann Fritz Fliegel.

Hauptmann Fritz Fliegel (second from the left) and his crew. Left to right are Leutnant Ernst Burkard, Fliegel, Unteroffizier Karl Maurer, Feldwebel Johannes Rottke, Unteroffizier Hans Kothe, and Gefreiter Karl Becker.

Unloading a Condor on return from a mission, Mérignac, early 1941.

Oberleutnant Heinrich Schlosser of 2/KG 40 in the cockpit of his Condor. He would be awarded the Ritterkreuz on 18 September 1941, and was later transferred to 10(Erg)/KG 40 to be an instructor.

Coded F8+AL and photographed at Mérignac in 1941, this aircraft shows quite a number of operational flights in addition to eleven shipping successes recorded on the rudder. In February 1941, this aircraft was flown four times by Hauptmann Bernhard Jope, the Staffel Kapitän of 3/KG 40.

Opposite: Hauptmann Hans-Jürgen Willers (left) was an experienced pilot who started the war flying He 111s with 4/KG 54. On 21 April 1940, he was shot down off the coast of Denmark and exactly a month later was wounded in action over Calais. After recovering from his wounds, he commanded Ergänzungsstaffel/KG 28 and then 10/KG 40. This photograph was taken when he was posted in December 1942, from 11/KG 40, to command KGzbv 200 in Russia. In the background is a very experienced Condor Fw 200 C-2, Wk Nr 0016, coded NA+WI, which arrived on 1/KG 40 on 10 July 1940. It was used occasionally by Hauptmann Daser before being transfered to 3/KG 40 in 1941; it was then relegated to Fw 200 crew training with IV./KG 40, serving as F8+BV, and then, as F8+BW, with 11 and 12/KG 40. The aircraft became a total loss on 21 May 1944 when it was strafed by USAAF fighters while under maintenance in the Lufthansa workshops at Leipzig-Schkeuditz airfield.

Another successful Condor seen at Mérignac in early 1941, this time with thirteen operational missions and ten shipping successes. Condor numbers were so low that such successes were credited to the aircraft, not the pilot. The dates are 16 December 1940, 11 January 1941, 20 February 1941 (3), 22 February 1941 (3), 27 February 1941 and 4 March 1941.

Work being carried out on a Fw 200 C-3 at Mérignac.

Carrying out engine runs on a Fw 200 C-3 at a wet Mérignac in January or February 1941. It is believed that this is F8+EK of 2/KG 40.

Further scenes at a wet Mérignac in January or February 1941.

Opposite above: Working on Fw 200 C-3 coded F8+AB of Stab I/KG 40, late 1941. Note the name *Mars* on the nose.

Opposite below: Condor F8+AB pictured in the air. Note the mission symbols and shipping successes marked on the tail and rudder. It is believed that this aircraft was the replacement for Wk Nr 0043, which had been lost in action on 18 July 1941. F8+AB would probably have been flown by the Gruppen Kommandeur, Hauptmann Edmund Daser.

Members of a Condor crew don their 10-76B kapok life preservers. The comparative space inside the aircraft and the fact that the life preserver did not require inflating made it popular with Condor crews. The lack of warm flying clothing being worn by most of the men in this photograph would indicate that it was taken in the summer and possibly on a non-operational flight.

Opposite above: The aircraft commander, or First Pilot, sat in the left-hand seat of a Condor.

Opposite below: Four engines meant that the Condors' instrument panels were crowded.

Fw 200 C-3 F8+DB of Stab I/KG 40. Note the sealed panel joints under the nose.

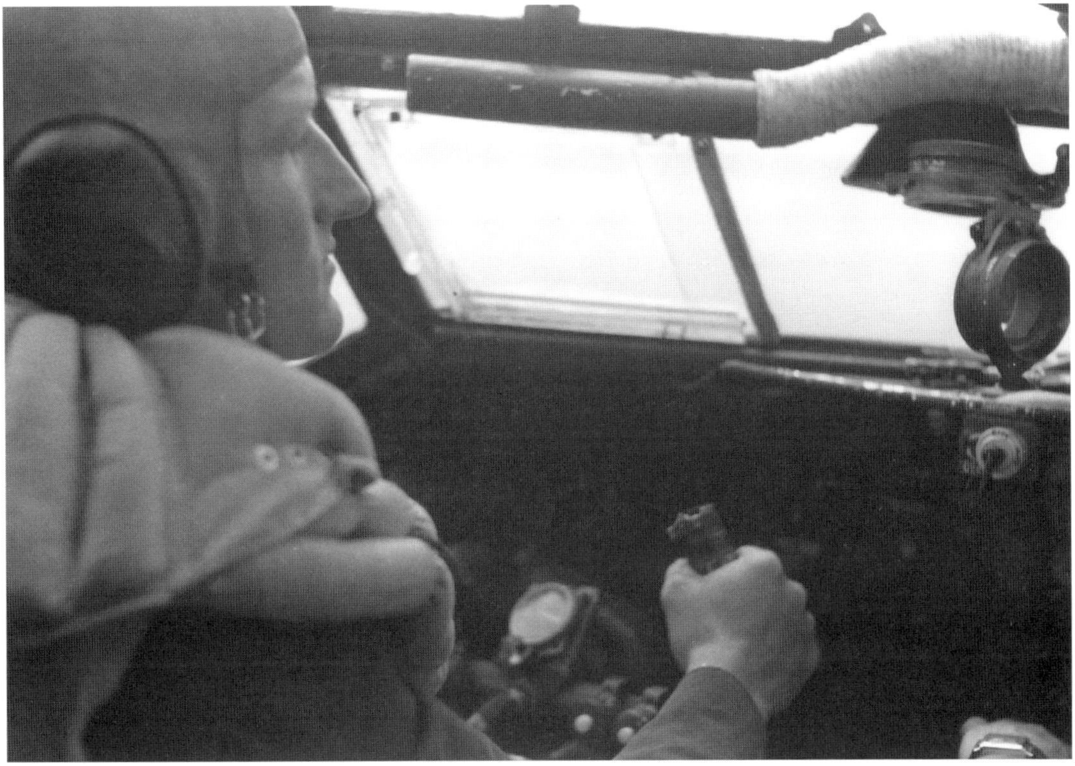

Drehen
Ziehen

Below and opposite: The first pictures in a dramatic series that show an unidentified crew carrying out a practice attack on the abandoned 8,571-ton SS *Flandre* in the Gironde Estuary, 1941.

Below and opposite: The closeness of the target to the Condor crew is graphically illustrated in these two images from the series.

Looking back at the target as the Condor departs the scene.

Condors ranged from one end of Europe to the other. This is a view of the Lofoten Islands in Norway as witnessed by one crew.

A Condor at low-level, well within Spanish territorial waters, in September 1941.

Opposite above: This is Mount Beerenberg on Jan Mayen Island, a volcanic island in the Arctic Ocean.

Opposite below: Two Condors over northern Iceland. Such incursions resulted in the USAAF basing fighters in the south and north of Iceland and a number of successes were achieved.

Opposite above: A Condor stalks a convoy out of range of its defences.

Opposite below: Internal long-range tanks gave the Condor an endurance of between fourteen and eighteen hours depending on bomb load.

The first of a series of photographs that depict the attack on an Allied convoy by Oberleutnant Franz Vüllers of 3/KG 40 on 19 March 1941.

Another picture from the series depicting Oberleutnant Franz Vüllers' attack on 19 March 1941. That day he had taken off from Mérignac at 02.35 hours at the controls of F8+GH; he landed at Stavanger at 14.52 hours.

During his attack on the convoy on 19 March 1941, Vüllers claimed to have sunk the 5,193-ton SS *Benvorlich*. A British cargo steamer built in 1919 by Charles Connell & Company, Scotstoun, *Benvorlich* went down west of Malin Head while on passage from Middlesbrough to the Far East. Twenty of her crew were lost.

The last of the images depicting Oberleutnant Franz Vüllers' attack on the convoy on 19 March 1941. He returned to Mérignac the following day without reporting any further success.

Thirty-one-year-old Leutnant Franz Vüllers seen at Mérignac in early 1941. He would be killed in an accident on a training flight on the night of 12-13 December 1941, when his Fw 200 C-3, Wk Nr 0055 coded F8+HK, crashed at Cognac; his death occurred shortly after his thirty-second birthday and four days after he was awarded the Ehrenpokal.

A Fw 200 C-4 (note the distinctive HDL 151 turret in the A Stand position) which is believed to be coded F8+BK of 2/KG 40. Note also the FuG 216 Neptun air-to-surface vessel (ASV) antennae on the rear fuselage. The aircraft is positioned on a compass swinging base.

What appears to be a Fw 200 C-4 of 7/KG 40, this aircraft is fitted with FuG Rostock ship search radar – note the antennae on the nose and wing tips. In the foreground are a mixture of 50kg and 250kg bombs.

This Condor, believed to be F8+GL of 3/KG 40, which was flown by Oberleutnant Franz Vüllers, has returned to Cognac on 13 August 1941 – along with a Parachute and Cable device fired from a ship that it was attacking.

Opposite: Oberleutnant Franz Vüllers, on the left wearing the peaked cap, and Hauptmann Bernhard Jope, wearing the peaked cap on the right, take a closer look at the Parachute and Cable device.

The FdF operated ten Condors of various versions. This is Fw 200 C-4/U2 Wk Nr 0138, coded CE+IC, which eventually crashed at Wilhelmsdorf near Potsdam on 27 April 1945. The aircraft carries a yellow fuselage band and on the nose is the FdF badge of an eagle's head.

Opposite above: Groundcrew working on a Condor give a good idea of its size.

Opposite below: KG 40's 'World in a Ring' emblem neatly depicts all the regions over which the Condor flew.

Originally Fw 200 A-0 Wk Nr 3098 D-ACVH named *Grenzmark*, this aircraft became NK+NM and was lost in an accident at Orel in the Soviet Union on 23 November 1941, whilst being operated by FdF. Note the Messerschmitt Bf 110 of Schnellkampfgeschwader 210 (which two months later formed Zerstörergeschwader 1) in the background with its distinctive wasp badge on the nose.

A clear photograph of a I/KG 40 Fw 200 C-3 which was taken at Mérignac in the summer of 1941. In the background are the distinctive aircraft hangars at his base. The aircraft has been fitted with the Kärcher Heizung, as evidenced by the intake below the turret.

A line up of five Condors of I/KG 40 at Mérignac, pictured in July 1941. All appear to be C-3 variants, but the 'World in a Ring' emblem has been removed by the censor who has also made reading the codes extremely difficult. The second aircraft appears to be F8+BA of Stab I/KG 40. Just visible on the nose of the nearest aircraft is the name *Elektra*. This aircraft was coded F8+EH.

Opposite above: A crew, believed to be from 7/KG 40, walk to their Condor. Note the FuG Rostock aerials just visible. All crew members are wearing 10-76B kapok life preservers, whilst the individual second from the right has binoculars around his neck. The heavily camouflaged hangars would indicate this photograph was taken later in the war when Allied day and night intruder aircraft were active.

Opposite below: Loading a 250kg bomb to a Fw 200 C-3 of I/KG 40. Note the name *Mars* on the nose – this aircraft was later coded F8+AB of Stab I/KG 40. In the background is either F8+DK or F8+DL of 2 or 3/KG 40.

A Fw 200 C-4 of III/KG 40. The white spinner tips could indicate 7 Staffel. Note the distinctive HDL 151 turret and the absence of a 'World in a Ring' emblem.

Snow on the ground could indicate the reason why this Fw 200 C-3 has come off the runway. The date and exact cause are not known.

Below and opposite: Identified by the HDL 151 turret, this is a Fw 200 C-4. This aircraft appears to have come off the runway, probably in Norway. The aircraft is also fitted with FuG Rostock, the aerials being just about visible in the image on the right.

The HDL 151 hydraulic dorsal turret gave the gunner good all-round visibility whilst the MG 151/20 cannon gave him good firepower. Note the compass markings around the turret which would allow the gunner to report with ease the bearing of a target or threat.

Oberleutnant Hans-Joachim Hase of 1/KG 40. In the background is Fw 200 C-2 Wk Nr 0017, coded NA+WJ. This aircraft was still serving with 11/KG 40 as late as 2 January 1943, when it was reported to have collided with a Fw 58 on landing at Berlin-Staaken airfield and suffered forty per cent damage. Hase was awarded the Ehrenpokal on 8 December 1941. He was shot down by Grumman Martlets of 802 Naval Air Squadron, operating from HMS *Audacity*, near Convoy HG 76 off Portugal on the 19th of the same month. He was flying Fw 200 C-3/U4 Wk Nr 0086, coded F8+IH, and he and his crew (Oberfeldwebel Karl Gendner, Oberfeldwebel Karl Bock, Unteroffizier Wilhelm Müller, Unteroffizier Robert Cordes and Gefreiter Raimund Steinke) were all killed.

The nearest aircraft is Fw 200 V3 Wk Nr 3099 coded 26-00 *Immelmann III* pictured whilst being operated by the FdF. It was later destroyed in an air raid on 18 July 1944. The occasion is believed to be Hitler's and Mussolini's visit to Heeresgruppe Süd and the Italian Army Corps at Uman in the Ukraine on 28 August 1941.

Fw 200 A-0 Wk Nr 3098, coded NK+NM, of FdF showing the additional intake on the nose peculiar to the earlier FdF Condors. This aircraft was destroyed in a crash-landing at Orel on 23 December 1941.

PART III

1942–1943

A Fw 200 C-4, that coded F8+GT, of 9/KG 40 photographed at Mérignac during 1942 or 1943.

This Fw 200 C-4 was probably photographed in 1943 as just visible on the tail is a fuselage band – yellow for Eastern Front, white for Mediterranean.

Opposite: A group of Fw 200 C-4s photographd at Mérignac. Note the Ju 88s, possibly Ju 88 C-6s from V/KG 40, in the background.

Above and opposite: Groundcrew working on a Condor.

Two views of Condors undergoing maintenance. The aircraft below is F8+GH of 1./KG 40.

An unusual view of Fw 200 C-3/U4 Wk Nr 0072. The factory code KF+QL became F8+CH of 1/KG 40.

The view from the First Pilot's window showing a Condor's port outer engine.

A war-weary Fw 200 C-3, that coded F8+CL, of 3/KG 40. It is thought that this is Wk Nr 0046. Flown by Leutnant Robert Maly, this aircraft suffered a technical defect on 9 July 1941, resulting in thirty per cent damage during a landing at Cognac. After its repair, it was re-coded F8+FL and then transferred to III/KG 40. It was finally abandoned in Russia on 16 January 1943 as part of KGzbV 200. Maly would be awarded the Deutsches Kreuz in Gold and survive the war.

This photograph of a Fw 200 C-4 of 9/KG 40, that coded F8+FT, was taken over the Bay of Biscay during 1943.

The aerials visible on the nose reveal that this III/KG 40 Fw 200 C-4 is fitted with FuG Rostock. It is also carrying 250kg bombs under the wings.

Two Fw 200 C-3s of I/KG 40 on the prowl over the Bay of Biscay. As Allied defences improved, low-level attacks were suspended for higher-level missions.

Towards the end of 1942, III/KG 40 became involved in resupply missions for the Afrika Korps, flying from Lecce in Italy. This image shows a 9/KG 40 crew after munitions have been unloaded.

Unloading fuel from F8+CT of 9/KG 40. Seen left to right are Unteroffizier Karl Nothelfer (killed on 27 January 1944 when the Condor in which he was flying was shot down by a de Havilland Mosquito intruder of 418 Squadron near Avord), Unteroffizier Siegfried Hoffmann and Unteroffizier Otto Kipp. The F8 appears to have been deliberately obscured.

Opposite: Personnel from 9/KG 40 in front of a Condor of Stab III/KG 40, coded F8+AD, in North Africa during the winter of 1942-43. Note the white Mediterranean fuselage band.

Opposite above: This Fw 200 C-4, F8+BT of 9./KG 40, ran short of fuel whilst returning from a transport mission and force-landed at Galatina in Italy on 19 November 1942. Leutnant Gerhard Pollmann and his crew were uninjured.

Opposite below: Bearing the same code as in the previous picture, the fuselage band of this Fw 200 C-4, seen at Benghazi in the autumn/winter of 1942-43, is positioned differently.

A Fw 200 C-3, that coded F8+DH, of 1/KG 40. It is unknown where this photograph was taken, but the aircraft carries a white fuselage band indicative of being involved in resupply missions at the end of 1942. Note the combat mission markings on the tail.

Fw 200 C-4s of I/KG 40 at Lecce in the autumn/winter of 1942-43. The aircraft carry white cowlings, white tail bands and the tips of the spinners are white.

Carrying passengers as well as freight is this Fw 200 C-3 of III/KG 40 destined for Lecce. Note the vehicle appears to be a captured British one.

Still in Africa, and seen left to right, are Unteroffizier Walter Spenrath (killed in an accident with 12/KG 40 on 18 July 1944), unidentified, Unteroffizier Hermann Neuwith and Unteroffizier Siegfried Hoffmann of 9/KG 40.

Unteroffizier Walter Spenrath and Unteroffizier Otto Kipp. In the background is a Junkers Ju 52 believed to be from III/KGzbV 1. It carries the tactical code T5. The Condor's spinner tip colours appear to be yellow.

A view of Fw 200 C-3 Wk Nr 0049 coded F8+FW. Flying with 1/KGzbV 200, it suffered a fuselage break, due to being overladen, whilst landing at Sslawjanskaja having returned from Saporoshje during the Stalingrad airlift in January 1943. Its pilot, Oberfeldwebel Werner Böck, would be reported missing over the Atlantic on 24 March 1943, whilst flying Fw 200 C-4, Wk Nr 0192, F8+ER, of 7/KG 40121.

A Fw 200 C-3, coded F8+CR, of 7/KG 40 seen in Norway winter 1942-43. It would be replaced by a Fw 200 C-4, Wk Nr 0147, also coded F8+CR, which was shot down over the Bay of Biscay on 13 June 1943.

This Fw 200 Condor of KGzbV 200 is believed to have been captured by the Soviets after the Stalingrad airlift in 1943. It is possible that this is C-3 0034, which was coded F8+GW.

A well-travelled Fw 200 C-4 Wk Nr 0097. With the factory code KE+IV, and serving with 3/KG 40, it suffered ten per cent damage in an air attack on Vaernes on 8 September 1942. This Condor was eventually written off following an accident in Nautsi, Finland, in 1944.

Refuelling what appears to be a Fw 200 C-3 at Mérignac.

Opposite: Fw 200 C-4/U2 Wk Nr 0181, coded GC+SJ, of the FdF. In addition to the FdF eagle, it carried a U-boat badge and the name *Albatross III*. This was the personal aircraft of Grossadmiral Dönitz and was captured at Flensburg at the end of the war. In RAF hands it became AIR MIN 97. It crashed on take-off from Schleswig airfield on 28 February 1946, and was scrapped shortly afterwards.

Fw 200 C-4 Wk Nr 0111 of 2/KG 40 suffered sixty per cent damage in an accident on take-off from Vaernes on 23 August 1942. It is believed that the factory code was NT+BK and that the aircraft also carried the code F8+BK.

ALBATROS

Three Fw 200 C-4s of III/KG 40. The nearest aircraft appears to be F8+AR, the middle one F8+DR of 7/KG 40, and the furthest F8+CD of Stab III/KG 40.

The last moments of a Fw 200C-4 of 7/KG 40, that with the Wk Nr 0186 and which was coded F8+ER. Intercepted by Bristol Beaufighters of 248 Squadron, it was shot down into the Atlantic at 10.01 hrs on 12 March 1943. The crews involved were Sergeant P. Wilkinson/Sergeant S. Bertram, Sergeant C. Goodwin/Sergeant W.J. Perry, Flying Officer C.R. Schofield/Sergeant J.A. Mallinson and Flying Officer R.C. Stringer/Pilot Officer S. Hunter. The Condor's crew of Leutnant Ernst Rabolt, Oberfeldwebel Alfred Lauer, Oberfeldwebel Hans Schmidt, Obergefreiter Alfred Beier, Oberfeldwebel Hans Stöckl and Obergefreiter Paul Florenkowski were all killed.

Another victim of the Beaufighters of 248 Squadron was Fw 200 C-4 Wk Nr 0132 which, coded F8+CK, was shot down on 29 July 1943. It ditched at position 45.30N 06.06W at 12.19 hours.

F8+CK was intercepted whilst attacking Convoy SL 133/MKS 18 by the Beaufighters crewed by Flying Officer P.A.S. Payne/Flying Officer A.M. McNicholl, Flying Officer G.C. Newman/Flying Officer C.C. Cochrane, Flying Officer F. Lacy/Warrant Officer G.C. Harker and Flying Officer J.K. Thompson/ Sergeant G.F. Barnes.

Two final views of F8+CK sinking after being shot down on 29 July 1943. The pilot, Oberfeldwebel Alfred Bolfrass, and a gunner, Unteroffizier Wilhelm Hahnstadt, were both killed, whilst the remainder of the crew, Unteroffizier Hans Gnuechtel, Gefreiter Siegfried Damm, Oberfeldwebel Rudolf Schöwe, Unteroffizier Herbert Kalus and Oberfeldwebel Wilhelm Holzhauer, survived the crash and were captured.

Apart from I, III and IV/KG 40 and FdF, very few other units operated the Fw 200. This was the sole Fw 200 C-3 operated by Blindflugschule 6 (BFS 6). Coded SG+KM, it had previously flown with I/KG 40 and carried two ship successes on the rudder and a line of 'England' mission markings. The badge on the nose is a black and white cow on a circle of red and orange quarters. BFS 6, reformed in June 1941 at Wesendorf, was responsible for training reconnaissance crews. In October 1943, it became BFS 36 and was disbanded a year later.

A picture of Fw 200 C-4 Wk Nr 0095 of Stab III/KG 40, coded F8+CD, which was being flown by Oberleutnant Joachim Ohm (the Gruppe Ia or Operations Officer), taken from a Condor flown by Oberleutnant Herbert Fobker. F8+CD was lost whilst being operated by KGzbV 200 on 19 January 1943. It was participating in the Stalingrad airlift at the time. Both Ohm and Fobker would be awarded the Deutsches Kreuz in Gold, the former surviving the war, the latter killed in a bombing raid on Cognac on 31 December 1943.

Opposite above: The view out of the waist gunner's position in a Condor. This weapon is an MG 17.

Opposite below: The MG 131 gave much better firepower as it used 13mm ammunition.

Opposite: The burning *Duchess of York* having been attacked on the evening of 11 July 1943 by Hauptmann Helmut Liman, Oberleutnant Ludwig Progner and Oberleutnant Egon Scherret of 7/KG 40. Liman would be killed in action on 27 September 1944 having returned to DLH; Scherrett would be interned in Ireland having force-landed there on 13 December 1943. Progner would be awarded the Deutsches Kreuz in Gold and survived the war. It is believed that Liman also received this award.

A Condor gets airborne.

A Fw 200 C-5/FK laden with two Hs 293 bombs. This is Wk Nr 0226, coded DP+ON, which was photographed whilst it was taking part in trials at Erprobungsstelle Karlshagen in 1943.

Opposite above: This picture of a Fw 200 C-8, that coded TO+XO, clearly shows the FuG 200 Hohentweil radar antennae. The aircraft was also equipped with the FuG 203b Kehl III missile control transmitter and was capable of being fitted with Henschel Hs 293 missiles.

Opposite below: A brand-new Fw 200 C-8 Wk Nr 0256 which has been converted to be a Fw 200 C-5/FK for Hs 293 operations. Clearly visible is the cabin heating system inlet and Hohentweil antennae. Defensive weapons have not yet been fitted.

Above and opposite below: This aircraft appears to be a captured Fw 200 C-5/FK, with the possible Wk Nr 0247 stencilled underneath the nose.

Opposite above: The Hs 293 guided bomb carried a 1,100lb warhead. A small rocket motor accelerated the missile to about 370mph which cut out after twelve seconds and the bomb coasted into its target in a shallow glide, again guided by a bomb aimer who was also aided by a small flare in the tail of the bomb.

Opposite: This Fw 200 C-4, Wk Nr 0173 and coded GC+SB, is fitted with FuG Rostock, the antennae being much thinner than the FuG 200 Hohentweil. On 18 March 1943, and whilst with I/KG 40, this aircraft suffered twenty per cent damage when it was forced to crash-land at Vaernes due to technical problems encountered on an operational sortie.

An almost pristine Fw 200, believed to be a C-4 variant.

Happier times for the Condor crews – a Fw 200 C-4 is close escorted by Junkers Ju 88 C-6s of V/KG 40 over the Bay of Biscay in the summer of 1943.

On 13 August 1943, Fw 200 C-5/U1 Wk Nr 0221 (TA+MW) of 9/KG 40 had a running battle with a Consolidated B-24 Liberator of the 1st Squadron of the 480th Anti-Submarine Group captained by Lieutenant Fred McKinnon. The Condor, flown by Oberleutnant Günther Seide, force-landed at Camarinas in Spain at 18.30 hours and was photographed by the victorious American crew.

Another view of TA+MW after it force-landed in Spain on 13 Auust 1943. Seide and his crew (Feldwebel Hans Greiwe, Feldwebel Gerhard Drews, Unteroffizier Werner Zerrahn, Oberfeldwebel Hans Böing, Obergefreiter Heinz Wagner and Unteroffizier Kurt von Au) soon returned to their unit. Seide would be killed in an accident on 11 May 1944.

Obergefreiter Lammers, Unteroffizier Hischfeld, Oberleutnant Helmut Liedtke (instructor), Feldwebel Hans Gensch and Unteroffizier Thomé, part of the crew of Leutnant Hans Harms, photographed at Orleans, whilst serving in 11/KG 40, during April 1942. Gensch was killed on 23 August 1943 when a Fw 200 C-5 of 9/KG 40, that with the Wk Nr 0214 and coded F8+NT (TA+MP), ditched in the Bay of Biscay. Oberfeldwebel Alfred Billing and the rest of the crew were rescued; Billing and two others were later killed flying a Heinkel He 177 from 2/KG 40 during an attack on London on 22 January 1944.

Opposite above: The shadow of Oberleutnant Joachim Ohm's F8+CD having just got airborne from Mérignac on 15 August 1943. This is another image taken as the Condors were heading out to intercept and attack Convoy OS 53/KMS 23.

Opposite below: Oberleutnant Arzinger closes in on Oberleutnant Ohm's Condor on 15 August 1943. Note the Hohentweil antennae on the nose. Arzinger would be awarded the Ehrenpokal and survived the war.

A Fw 200 C-6 of Stab III/KG 40, Wk Nr 0218 and coded F8+AD (TA+MT), pictured having just taken off from Mérignac on the afternoon of 15 August 1943. It was commanded by Oberleutnant Alfred Arzinger. That day, twenty-one Condors, led by the recently-appointed Geschwader Kommodore and former Gruppen Kommandeur of III/KG 40, Major Robert Kowalewski, had been detailed to attack Convoy OS 53/KMS 23. This Condor crashed at Malvik, near Drontheim, during a training flight on 14 August 1944. Oberleutnant Rudolf Biberger (Gruppen Adjutant) and five crew members were killed; just one man survived.

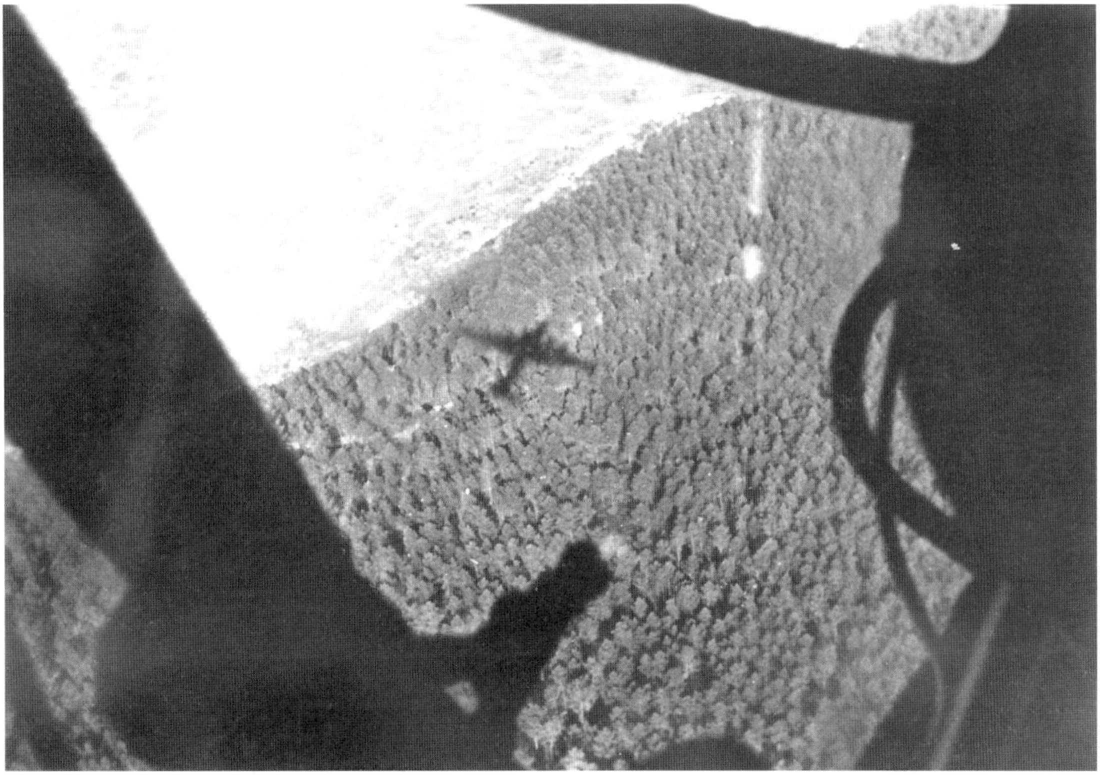

Oberleutnant Arzinger's F8+AD has pulled back; two more Condors are seen to the starboard of the formation.

Oberleutnant Ohm has moved to the port of the Kette; ahead is Major Kowalewski's C-6 F8+AA (possibly Wk Nr 0210 formerly TA+ML) and to the starboard is Oberleutnant Arzinger's Condor. Kowalewski was a recipient of the Ritterkreuz and survived the war.

Two further views of the formation of Condors as it climbs to altitude and heads for the convoy on 15 August 1943.

The Condors located the ships of Convoy OS 53/KMS 23 some 220 miles north-west of Lisbon, at which point they launched their attack. Despite then number of aircraft involved, only one vessel, the SS *Warfield* (ninety-four crew were rescued but two killed), was sunk, whilst two others were damaged.

The Condors did not escape unscathed on 15 August 1943. Oberleutnant Bernhard Kunisch force-landed his Fw 200 C-4, Wk Nr 0166, coded F8+ER (CH+CG), at Lavacolla, near Santander in Spain, having been damaged by flak from HMS *Stork*. He and his crew returned to France. Along with four of his crew from the actions against Convoy OS 53/KMS 23, he was shot down and killed by Mosquitoes of 248 Squadron on 20 November 1943.

A group photograph of Condor crewmen. Fourth from the left is Hauptmann Georg Schabert of 7/KG 40. He is possibly standing in front of Fw 200 C-5 Wk Nr 0222, which was coded F8+AR (TA+MX). This aircraft was shot down by Beaufighters of 248 Squadron at 15.29 hours on 20 November 1943. At the time it was commanded by Oberleutnant Bernhard Kunisch. As for Hauptmann Georg Schabert, he and his crew (Oberfeldwebel Wilhelm Friedrichs, Oberfeldwebel Kurt Scheunert, Feldwebel Paul Böber, Unteroffizier Erwin Pauli, Feldwebel Johann Aixner, Unteroffizier Fritz Lautenschläger and Unteroffizier Siegfried Radauer) were reported missing over the Atlantic on 29 December 1943. At the time they were flying Fw 200 C-8 (C-5/FK) Wk Nr 0246, coded F8+IR (TO+XB), on a Hs 293 mission.

This Fw 200 C-6 of 7/KG 40, Wk Nr 0237 and coded F8+MR (TK+CS), force-landed at Drominseer in County Tipperary, Ireland, on 13 December 1943. It had been damaged by flak during operations against an Allied convoy. Oberleutnant Egon Scherret and Second Pilot Unteroffizier Hans Meindl successfully crash-landed, after which they set fire to the aircraft. (Irish Air Corps)

Another view of the wreckage of F8+MR (TK+CS) at Drominseer. Scherret and Meindl, together with Unteroffizier Karl-Heinz Schwarzkopf, Feldwebel Hans Rassek, Unteroffizier Ulrich Winkler, Oberfeldwebel Wilhelm Voll, Feldwebel Alfred Thiemt and Unteroffizier Bruno Arndt, were all interned. (Irish Air Corps)

PART IV
1944–1945

Opposite: From mid-1944 onwards, Condors were increasingly used for basic transportation roles and when KG 40 was disbanded, in November 1944, 8/KG 40, commanded by Hauptmann Ludwig Progner, formed Transportfliegerstaffel Condor and operated from Norway. Judging by the passengers wearing civilian clothing, this C-3 is being used in the transport role.

Fw 200 C-4 Wk Nr 0097 (KE+IV) was serving with 3/KG 40 in September 1942. Coded F8+CS, it was eventually written off following an accident in Nautsi, Finland, on 17 October 1944 when it suffered an engine failure on take-off. The pilot, Oberfeldwebel Willi Bergen, was injured.

In this second image of the wreckage of F8+CS at Nautsi, it is possible to note the Wk Nr 0097 on the front of the gondola and the remains of a Hohentweil array. Although stated to be a 3 Staffel aircraft, the markings actually indicate 8 Staffel; but it is believed that by this time it was serving with Transportfliegerstaffel Condor.

Photographed at Vaernes on 8 April 1944, in front of F8+FL of 3/KG 40, is Oberleutnant Karl-Heinz Stahnke's crew celebrating his 600th operational flight. Stahnke was a very experienced transport pilot who converted to the Condor in the spring of 1943. He came to even greater prominence for his daring rescue mission of weather station personnel from Franz Josef Land in the Arctic in July 1944, after which he was awarded the Ritterkreuz on 24 October of that year. This was followed by the Ritterkreuz mit Eichenlaub on 27 March 1945. From left to right in this picture are Unteroffizier Max Resler, Leutnant Werner Bohnstedt, Unteroffizier Heinz Krichhoff, unidentified, Stahnke, Feldwebel Reinhold Wechsler, and another unidentified individual.

In late 1944, a number of Condors were transferred to 14/Transportgeschwader 4 at Wiener-Neustadt in Austria, where two formed a Sonderkommando commanded by Oberleutnant Karl-Heinz Stahnke. The precise purpose of this unit is unknown, though it may have been part of preparations for an attack on the Suez Canal with Hs 293s. At 23.45 hours on 30 March 1945, Stahnke took off from Wiener Neustadt in G6+AY bound for Calato on Rhodes, arriving just before dawn on 31 March. Later that day, six Bristol Beaufighters of 252 Squadron, which were based at Hassani in Greece, took off with the intent of destroying the German aircraft at Calato. On arriving at the target, the RAF crews reported finding no aircraft, so promptly attacked buildings on the airfield with cannon fire. However, on developing camera gun film after their return, this heavily camouflaged Condor was identified among the olive trees.

At the end of the war, Condors were discovered at numerous airfields across Europe. F8+FS was a Fw 200 C-5/FK of Transportfliegerstaffel Condor which was captured at Achmer on 8 May 1945. It was being flown by Oberfeldwebel Willi Bergen, who had been tasked to undertake a transport mission from Vaernes to Kurland, when it was diverted to Wuppertal in Germany but in fact landed at Achmer. Interestingly, Bergen had previously been injured in the crash of Wk Nr 0097 on 17 October 1944. Repainted in RAF markings, this aircraft was believed to have been seen at Melsbroek in Belgium, but its eventual fate is unknown. Like all the others it was no doubt scrapped shortly afterwards.

This is believed to be a Fw 200 C-6, that coded F8+UL, of 3/KG 40. The photograph was taken over Norway in 1944.